WHATEVER IT TAKES

Walking Through God's Purpose

SHELDON THERAGOOD

Cocoon to Wings
PUBLISHING

Printed in the United States of America
ISBN: 978-1-953497-15-4 (Paperback)
ISBN: 978-1-953497-16-1 (Digital)

Library of Congress Control Number: 2021908044

Published by Cocoon to Wings Publishing
7810 Gall Blvd, #311
Zephyrhills, FL 33541
www.CocoontoWingsBooks.com
(813) 906-WING (9464)

Scriptures marked KJV are taken from the KING JAMES VERSION (KJV):
KING JAMES VERSION, public domain.

Scriptures marked NLT are taken from the HOLY BIBLE NEW LIVING
TRANSLATION (NLT): Scriptures taken from the HOLY BIBLE, NEW
LIVING TRANSLATION, Copyright ©1996, 2000, 2002, 2003 by Holman
Bible Publishers, Nashville Tennesee. All rights reserved.

Scriptures marked ESV are taken from THE HOLY BIBLE, ENGLISH
STANDARD VERSION (ESV): Scriptures taken from THE HOLY BIBLE,
ENGLISH STANDARD VERSION ® Copyright© 2001 by Crossway, a
publishing ministry of Good News Publishers. Used by permission.

Book design by ETP Creative

WHATEVER IT TAKES

CONTENTS

In Loving Memory of
Helen Theragood Woodard aka "Memaw"

ACKNOWLEDGMENTS

First, I'd like to give glory to God for allowing me to experience challenges and helping me stay dedicated and loyal to my purpose while building a foundation for our future youth.

My Mother - thank you for motivating me and encouraging me not to give up and to stay focused on my vision.

My Grandmother - thank you for your prayers and always providing me with spiritual and inspirational words that have guided me throughout my life's journey.

My Sister - I appreciate you for always being a phone call away when I need you, for being a great listener, helping me come up with great ideas and for pushing me to be great.

TheraGood Deeds, Inc. - thank you for believing in me and making a vision come to pass.

Finally, thank you to all the writers who supported me throughout this process by helping me complete my mission of writing this book.

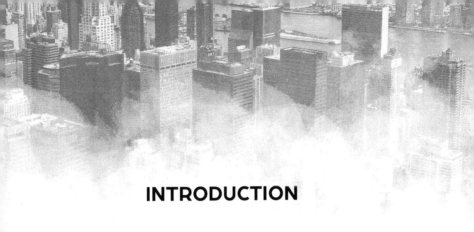

INTRODUCTION

Basketball was my passion and I thought that it was going to take me places. I excelled in it and received a ton of accolades. My older brother and his friends played basketball in the neighborhood. Since I wanted to be like him, it made sense that I would play basketball too. He practiced, so I practiced. He played high school ball, so I played high school ball. I wasn't as good as he was, but I grew into a skillful player just as great as he was. He was my motivator. There were always wonderful things said about him. He was a great shooter, but I became a better ball handler.

Although I didn't play in the NBA, basketball became the foundation my life was built on. It instilled in me many skills, such as being a great leader, working hard, and stepping out of my comfort zone. Those characteristics carried me from high school into my career as a police officer and helped me establish a non-profit organization, Theragood

Deeds. Basketball also kept me out of trouble as a teenager, helped me develop mental toughness, and provided me with life skills to successfully maneuver through all that life has thrown at me. The sport I still love helped me to find my purpose - helping troubled teens.

I am now walking in my God-given purpose, and it was the journey through sports that allowed me to discover it. Through sports, the mentors, and the skills I acquired, I saw a path toward greatness that I am not sure I would have found without it. In the next chapters, I intend to not only share with you how I found myself serving the young people of Houston, Texas, but how I was able to find my passion and do what I love. I hope to inspire you to do whatever it takes (#watevaittakes) to reach your goals and find your purpose.

MY NEIGHBORHOOD & FAMILY

Shepherd Park Terrace is the neighborhood I grew up in, beginning at the age of 13. My mom and dad had separated, so we moved in with my awesome maternal grandparents on the Northside of Houston, Texas. My grandfather was always supportive being at my little league games and would encourage me to do my best each time. He then got sick and quickly passed away. My grandmother did an amazing job raising me. I always referred to her as Grandma. I was blessed to have all my grandparents living at the time, but on different sides of town in Houston. While staying with my grandparents I attended F.M. Black Middle School and Scarborough High School. My older brother, my younger sister, and I grew up in the same household. When we moved to my grandparent's home, I knew I would have to find new friends and wouldn't have as much freedom as I did when my parents were together.

My grandma is my rock. She was a Sunday School teacher at her church, a nurse, even a preacher at times. I knew she was going to make me go to church living under her roof. Before you knew it, I had joined a church that was right around the block from the neighborhood. My grandma also instilled in me the power of prayer and how to build a relationship with God by saying prayers, reading the Bible, joining a church, giving thanks for waking me up in the morning, and giving me another opportunity to make a difference in someone's life. I always said my grandma and God must be best friends because she preached and prayed about Him all the time. I don't think there's ever been a time in a conversation she and I had that she didn't mention God. My grandma could go into the Bible and find a scripture that would help me solve any problems. She is my spiritual leader and encourages me always to say my prayers no matter what.

I also lived with my dad's mother and father, on the Southside of town. One of the main reasons why I loved going to my grandparent's home on the southside was because my grandfather would give me money and my grandmother, which we refer to her as Memaw, would make sure my stomach was full of food. She was an awesome cook and had her own catering business. My grandfather didn't play when it came to being disobedient, and he taught me how to become an awesome young man before he passed. While living with them, I attended high school at Jack Yates and college at Texas Southern University in Houston, Texas, which was within walking distance from where we lived. Spending time in the kitchen with my grandma and seeing how much she impacted the community with her cooking, really inspired me to be like her one day. She hardly ever slept because of how much she cared about other people and making sure her food orders were perfect and done on time. Funny fact about my Memaw is she never drove a vehicle in her life but was able to call and sweet talk anyone into taking her to the store to get her groceries. Her way of repaying you was treating you to a nice restaurant or even giving you money. And I've never known anyone to turn her down. My Memaw taught me how to be respectful and not talk back, be responsible, how to clean up and cook. There was no need to sit down if you were at her house because it was time to work or get cursed out. Anything related to discipline, Memaw's name was on it! She would love you and give you her last. You didn't have to worry about starving, and she definitely loved her grandkids. I was blessed to be raised right.

I also can't forget my amazing mother who cares so much about me. My mother is my heartbeat, and I would do anything for her. Even though I didn't make it to the NBA to get her that nice house, I know she's still proud of me. My mother also encouraged me to keep writing and not to give up and because of her, I was able to complete this book.

As I've mentioned, my older brother was my role model. He was always in the most fashionable clothing. He wasn't just good on the basketball court but an attractive, likable guy. When I was young, I would take his clothes after he left for school. Although he is four years older than me, when he went out to play basketball with friends, I always wanted to go too. But I knew because of my size and skill level, that I wasn't going to get picked. I wanted to go anyway. Whenever I didn't get a chance to play, I stood on the sideline taking notes and dribbling my basketball until he finally gave me a chance to play. He has always built great relationships with everyone around him, and I wanted to do the same thing on and off the court.

My dad, who people say I strongly resemble, started me off in little league sports. My dad really loved me and was so excited when I transferred to Jack Yates High School. It was a tradition and it made me proud to say that I graduated from the same high school as him; it was the best decision of my life. He always encouraged me saying, "Your time is coming; all the things you're doing for others will pay off."

My little sister watched me like I watched my older brother. Because I played basketball in high school, she did as well. I went to college at Texas Southern University; she did the same. I joined a fraternity; she joined a sorority. Pursuing my master's encouraged her to do the same. She saw something in me that she wanted to emulate and thank God I was a proper influence.

This amazing foundation of love, respect, discipline, values, and prayers influenced me and guided my future. It also instilled the desire to become that type of foundation for others who may be lacking it. God was grooming me for my role in life, even in my own upbringing.

The neighborhood where I grew up was quiet and everyone looked out for one another. Now we might have seen fights at times, but that was all. My neighborhood was a community full of family. I used to dribble the ball everywhere I went. I had a dream, like many little kids, to make it to the NBA. I was determined to work hard to make my dream come true. I dribbled the ball up one side of the street and down the other. All the neighbors on the block always knew where I was when they heard that sound. They also knew that basketball was my passion. Even as a young kid, I was motivated to do great things. I just didn't know at the time what they would be, and I was willing to do #watevaittakes to make that happen, even if that meant annoying everyone in the neighborhood by dribbling my basketball!

HOOP DREAMS

> "If you set your goals ridiculously high and it's a failure, you will fail above everyone else's success."
> ~ James Cameron, Film Maker, and Environmentalist

I became one of the top point guards in Houston and was known for my speed and amazing ball-handling skills. But basketball was not all about me. I did my best showing dedication and leadership to my teammates and coach playing the point guard's position. It was my duty to run the team's offense and maintain control of the ball. I didn't think I would get any taller, even though I had dreams of becoming seven feet tall. I would hang on the monkey bars because people told me that would make my arms stretch. I figured out that only made my arms hurt. I accepted that I would be 5 feet 8 inches for the rest of my life and just focused on being a great point guard.

Although I was less than six feet tall, I proved to onlookers that you don't have to be a giant to pursue your dreams. My dad put me in football, basketball, and baseball at an early age. Although I enjoyed all three sports, it became clear that my skill and talent were in basketball. I was so grateful I participated in all three because they had a major impact on my life and taught me how to work with others and become a leader. Playing sports also required demanding work and determination, which paid off when I was recruited by multiple colleges including the University of North Carolina-Wilmington (UNCW), Southern Methodist University (SMU), Oregon State University (OSU), and more. They all needed a point guard at the time. Unfortunately, I didn't make the scores to be accepted into the schools. At that point in my life, I did not understand the importance of education or preparing for what would lie ahead in life.

Thanks to my awesome high school coach at Jack Yates High School, I received a two-year basketball scholarship to play at Grayson College in Denison, TX. Although extremely grateful for this opportunity, I was not closer to my dream after the first basketball season at Grayson. I did not play to my fullest potential and incurred a minor hip injury. My coach was extremely hard on me, and I wasn't mentally strong enough to handle his coaching style. When I got into the game, my confidence was low, and therefore, my performance was poor. I lost confidence in myself, which was apparent during practices and games. One day I had an all-star game scoring 21 points with several assists, wishing I could keep that momentum up every game, but it didn't work out that way. The coach made me nervous as he was always fussing at me, which did not help my confidence. Unfortunately, I spent a good portion of that year on the bench.

No matter how things turned out on the court, college was a wonderful experience. I no longer had my mom waking me up, so I had to manage my own responsibilities, alarm clock, basketball practice, and class requirements. I was an adult learning how to manage every day. It was shocking to me because I was away from home. I had to get books, plan the semester's courses, avoid distractions. After finishing the season miserably, I decided to go back home and try my luck at Texas Southern University (TSU) in my hometown.

I transferred to Texas Southern University and lived with my Memaw. I was immediately blessed with a walk-on opportunity, which meant I wasn't recruited beforehand, and I didn't receive any athletic scholarship to play on the team. While playing there, I experienced that same pain in my hip that affected me at Grayson College. No matter how hard I played, the pain wouldn't go away. I started off on the right track deciding to work harder than anyone else on the team. And by doing so, I was acknowledged by our fitness coach, which then gave me the nickname "pound for pound." I outworked everyone. A couple of weeks of practice went by and I began slacking off. And the pain in my hips got worse. Coach then told me to get checked out by a doctor. I was diagnosed with osteoarthritis not only in one hip but both. This did not help my confidence in my physical abilities, that diagnosis was a life-changing blow to my ego. I assumed with this injury that I definitely was not going to make it to the Pros. Unfortunately, I didn't even make it on the team. Feeling defeated, I didn't want to talk to anyone. My dream was to play basketball in the NBA, so I didn't have a backup plan. Lesson learned. I should have realized that my chances of making it onto a professional court were slim. I should have developed an alternate plan of action. At that time, I couldn't see that far in advance. I began to think about all the games I played in the past, including those when my team lost. Those memories reminded me that I was a competitor and had to get my life back in the game, which meant I had to get serious about school and focus on graduating and getting a degree.

Since basketball was out of the picture, I had more time to dedicate to school, although that wasn't easy. I joined a fraternity, Kappa Alpha Psi Fraternity Inc. (KAY), and was having an awesome time living my best life. I loved the way they dressed, these guys got all the girls and made a lot of friends. Although they threw exciting parties on campus, their most important responsibility was leadership and taking care of the community. I wanted to be a part of that. They were leaders on the school campus, and I thought that was huge. There was so much happening on campus that you could easily miss a full day of classes! But I was determined to graduate, so I had to avoid distractions as best I could. Nothing was going to stop me from getting my education. However, they did have intramural basketball, which I could not resist playing. As thrilled as I was to be back on the court, I was still trying to get over not playing college ball. I decided to use the opportunity to show off my skills and prove that I should be on the college team.

I was happy about how good it felt to be playing ball again and even better - winning. I had lots of friends and was one of the coolest guys on "the yard," also known as the school campus. I was always happy and loved making others happy. I have a huge, sensitive heart, and I have always wanted to help other people. At the time, I did not know how those characteristics would help me to find my purpose.

Like many others at my age then, I made some good decisions and some bad ones that could have gotten me into trouble. I was trying to be cool and be part of the clique. I was young and ignorant and could have found myself in serious trouble with the law if not for the "what if" factor. For as long I can remember, my mom always asked, "what if?" "What if you hang around the wrong people?" "Be careful who you surround yourself with." She always reminded me to think before I react about a decision that could impact my life forever. I was trying to take advantage of being a young man in college, having an enjoyable time, being at an HBCU (Historically Black College and University) right in my backyard. But my mother's words were always at the back of my mind, "What if..." She used to tell me, "people who say they're your friends are not always your friends" or "A hard head makes a soft behind." Implementing the "what if" factor is a preventative way of helping you to not make the wrong decision. I believe this would be helpful for many youths out there who are dealing with the same temptations in their environment - drugs, criminal activities, that could potentially change their life for the worse.

Be careful and be conscious of how your decisions today could impact your life tomorrow.

I remember one night my friends and I decided to handle a situation. Here we were early twenties thinking we were full grown. Most of the guys that I hung around with had been in trouble with law enforcement. Some of us played basketball; we all dressed fly and attracted attention on the yard. I was trying to be cool, to stay in the circle. I had a vehicle, so I went out with them, being young and ignorant. In the car, I listened to them rattle on about what they were going to do. They never actually revealed their plan to me, but I figured it out. They were trying to rob someone at gunpoint. Once I realized what was about to happen, I gripped the steering wheel in fear. My heart was beating out of my chest. I felt warm on the inside like I was going to throw up. The other guys were telling me where to go. "Turn here. Go down this street." They gave directions and I drove. One of them in the backseat was holding a weapon. I was driving so fast. "Slow down!" That's what they said, but I did the complete opposite trying to pass the streets where they wanted me to coast with my headlights off. All the time I was praying no one would be on the street. *What did I get myself into? I want to go home. Man, I'm trippin'.* Nothing was going right. We were all nervous and scared. Apparently, the plan was to jack someone on the street. Literally no one was walking down the street. No one! To this day, I believe God had His angels around my vehicle because nothing happened at all. He kept people off the streets so that the mission could not be accomplished. I was relieved as I dropped them off and nervously drove home to sleep the night off.

I couldn't believe I had put myself in that situation after what my mother had taught me. I could hear my mom in my ear telling me to be careful with who I hang around with, and here I was calling out to her in my mind, *"Mama, where are you?"* I was so scared, my life flashed before me. What if we got caught? When I drove back to the house, I replayed the whole evening in my head, and I knew I had made a mistake. Even though nothing happened, it felt like I got in trouble. If I had gotten in trouble, I would have been locked up. My mom would have said, "I told you so." I could see the people who admired me at school looking at me differently because I would have a record. I went to bed that night asking myself, "What were you thinking?"

I was trying to be all hard and prove that I was tough. But not thinking, what if things had gone as they planned instead of how God planned it? I wouldn't have anything to show for my life. No one would have respected me anymore. How would my grandmothers have felt? No one would have wanted to hang with me. Those so-called friends should have told me, "This is not for you, bro!

Stay in your lane and do great things like you're destined to do!" But they didn't; so, it was up to me to make a wise decision. Thankfully, I'm able to use this tool to help me in the future, preventing me from making decisions that could certainly change my life trajectory.

I knew college graduation was coming soon, and I would do #watevaittakes to cross that stage and get my degree. And I knew that God had my back and other plans for me.

> **Keys to Success:**
>
> Understand that life is not always going to go your way, but with hard work and perseverance, your dreams can still come true.
>
> Use the "what if" factor in determining whether a decision will either keep you on the right path or lead you down a path that's not aligned with God's will for you.
>
> Always have a backup plan! Life will throw you curveballs and you have to be prepared for whatever is thrown at you.

A NEW START

> *"You never fail until you stop trying." ~ Albert Einstein, World-renown Inventor, and Physicist*

Well, the time had finally come for one of my dreams to come true... graduation day! I guess you can say all the hard work and utilizing my "what if" tool helped me stay on the right track and get to the finish line to walk across the stage and receive my college degree. I was so excited and couldn't wait to see my family and their happy faces, especially my little sister, who looked up to me and who was my heart. The "yard" was packed with people who couldn't wait to see their family members walk across the stage. It reminded me of the Maroon and Gray basketball game I played in at Texas Southern University when the new basketball team was introduced. Students couldn't wait to see how the team would look for the new year. I did not know at the time that I was going to be cut from the team, but it still felt so good to be out there listening to the roar of the crowd. This was also before I knew I needed a backup plan. Now, as I walked across that stage to receive my degree, listening to that same excitement of the crowd including my family, it struck me that although this had not been my original motivation, my backup plan was going to set me up for my next move in life. In basketball, you can endure a career-ending injury, and without a degree an athlete's options are limited. However, earning a degree stays with you forever, no matter what injury you have.

Basketball was a gift from God that brought me a mighty long way toward graduation day, and I thanked God for inviting the sport into my life. Little did I know the mental toughness I acquired while playing would be especially useful as I now had to figure out what my next move would be in finding a job, creating a life for myself, and finding my purpose. I was a competitor. I never gave up. I was still living the basketball life, but now those skills would come in handy as I entered real life.

After graduation from TSU with a Bachelor of Arts degree in Communications, I began focusing on the future, starting with getting a job. My first goal was to save enough money to get out of my Memaw's house, learn how to become a man and be responsible. I was ready to do #watevaittakes!

The first thing I did was to check out who was hiring. I did not know what I wanted to do, so I basically was looking for any J.O.B. Some of my friends said being a security guard was a solid job because it offered benefits and job security. Security job it is! I was fresh out of college with a college degree I could brag about. Being confident, having a great personality and great with people were qualities that were sure to seal the deal.

I went on a security application spree. I went to one place after another with my bright smile, head up and chest out, asking if anyone was hiring. I went to so many locations, yet I was determined. "One more location can't hurt." That's how I would encourage myself. The last company that I approached was near my home and paid a dollar more than the rest. So once again, with my bright smile, head up, and chest out, I walked inside asking if they were hiring for security positions. The guy at the front desk told me to give him a minute to get his supervisor. I took a deep breath because I really wanted that job. The supervisor came out, looked at me, and said, "You look familiar." He recognized me from college. We were glad to see each other, and because he knew me, he decided to hire me on the spot. He knew that I was a great basketball player who worked hard and put my heart and soul into the game. He knew that I would also do the same for the position. I guess it's true, "It's all about who you know." He then gave me the address to where to pick up my uniform. I was so thankful that I had always kept the idea that my future was at stake in all of my decisions. I was grateful to my mom for instilling the "what if" factor in me and that my conscious efforts had now led me to this next chapter in life.

It felt like it was graduation day all over again. As soon as I got home, I went straight to the mirror to see how I looked in my security uniform. I even thought I was "Topflight Security of the World" like Day-Day and Craig in the movie "Next Friday." I thought being a security guard was going to be a whole lot of fun. I had no way of knowing it would be the beginning of my career in law enforcement.

My first job assignment was at a chemical plant where I was stationed at the gate checking cars into the facility. During the heat of the Houston summer, I took every opportunity I could to escape to my little shack. Cars kept coming preventing me from enjoying the shade provided by that shack. "Man, all this for an extra dollar of pay," I said to myself as another car approached. I then contacted the Supervisor to see if I could get a new post. After talking to my supervisor, I was informed I had to wait several months before I could transfer. After three weeks, I couldn't take the heat anymore. I began to search for another job. I was more informed this time around and knew the questions to ask, so I didn't get stuck in a little shack in the dead of summer. I was determined - once again - to do whatever it took to find another job.

Keys to Success:

Don't give up! Just because one door shuts doesn't mean that another one will not open.

Be mindful of your demeanor and how you treat people because you never know who is watching.

Whether or not you decide to pursue a future in sports, education is critical in being able to obtain the job or career that you want.

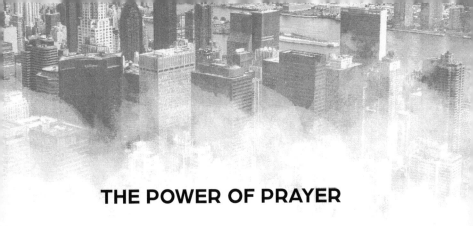

THE POWER OF PRAYER

> *"And we know that for those who love God all things work together for good, for those who are called according to his purpose." ~ Romans 8:28 (ESV)*

One Sunday morning, my grandma, a dedicated church-going woman, wanted me to visit her church. She said the people there would be happy to see me since it had been a while since I'd visited. It was mandatory to go to Sunday school and church as a little kid, although I didn't like my grandma's church because service seemed like it lasted the whole day. It was like working part-time at the security job! I confess Jesus Christ to be my Savior, and I love the Lord, but I think that to join my grandma's church you have to be at least 65 years old. For real! As I walked into the church that Sunday, everyone first hugged my grandmother and then asked, "Is this your grandson?"

"Wow, he done grew up!" These are the main two things everyone in the church says when they haven't seen you in a while (tell me if I'm wrong). "Yes, this is my grandson," my grandma confirmed.

Even though I didn't feel like I belonged in her church, she's the reason why I was able to establish a great relationship with God. Once we finally made our way over to our seats, one of the deacons shook my hand, genuinely glad to see me, but then he asked a deep question, one that would forever change my life. "Hey, son, what's your purpose in life?"

I stared at him in deep thought. I originally thought it was basketball. Like many other young athletes, I was sure that God's plan for my life MUST include playing on a professional court. Since that was clearly out of the picture, I had not considered what the plan for my life was.

"I don't know, sir. I thought it was basketball, but I didn't make the team."

"I'm not saying your hobby, son. What I mean is, what's the purpose that God has for you?"

I stared at him, and shook my head, "I don't know, Deacon."

The deacon replied, "It's okay, but keep that in mind, because if you don't know your purpose, you have to find it and trust me, you will. Talk with you later, and good seeing you."

I stood in the same spot with a blank stare as the deacon spoke with other church members.

Following the service, I drove home in deep thought about what the deacon asked. I decided to follow my grandma's advice and pray. I asked God, "What is my purpose, Lord? Please send one of your angels my way to tell me. I really want to know." I couldn't think of anything else I was passionate about other than playing basketball and helping kids improve their basketball game. Let me ask you the same question, "What is your purpose?" If you don't know it yet don't worry. Believe me when I say that God has a plan and purpose for everyone's life. It is predetermined and laid out for us before we are born. Our job is to figure out what it is.

The next morning, I was back on duty at my security job but scrolling through job boards on my phone. All I had in my mind was, "I have to find my purpose." In my heart, after my conversation with the deacon, I knew security work wasn't it. Soon a whole line of cars came to the gate. Although I was upset, I still jumped up with a smile on my face. I still respected everyone even though I was unhappy. So many people passed through my gate every day who were making big money; I thought, "One day, I know that will be me." If I stayed focused and believed in myself, there would be many opportunities for me. As the deacon said, I knew I would find my purpose.

Besides basketball, the only thing I had a passion for was helping kids, especially teaching them how to dribble the ball. I didn't want to be a schoolteacher. I wanted to teach but just not in the classroom. Teaching them how to play ball made me feel like I was back on the basketball court again. Each time I spoke, they listened to every word that came out of my mouth. I could tell they were eager to go out and get the job done. When I was playing, the coaches were excited and had fun doing what they love. You could see their excitement when they put a play in place, and we executed it.

Although sports teaches kids critical lessons, having fun is still the most important part. Yes, you must be serious about what you are doing, but you also want kids to have fun. This will make learning about life and how to make great decisions even easier for them. Coaching seemed to be a terrific way of giving back and helping others, which is what I learned from my grandparents. I also thought coaching would settle my frustration about not playing ball anymore. I needed to find a career that would hopefully help me figure out my purpose. I was clearly still struggling with basketball not being it. So, I continued to pray for guidance.

Keys to Success:

If you are unaware of what your purpose is, write down the things you feel strongly and passionate about to help you determine what it is.

Be willing to listen and take advice from others even when you prefer not to.

Whenever things don't go the way you plan, there's power in prayer so put it in God's hands. He will guide you where you need to be.

DREAMS COME TRUE

> *"All our dreams can come true if we have the courage to pursue them." ~ Walt Disney, Showman, Pioneer, and Creator*

Still surfing for available job opportunities, I found out that the Harris County Juvenile Detention Center was hiring for a Detention Officer. I met all the requirements; the only thing I had to do was pass a background check. I knew I was good as far as that was concerned. I realized that this opportunity might be in God's plan as it would be a way that I could help kids. Maybe God had bigger plans for me to help them that had nothing to do with basketball. Maybe I could share with them the many life skills I had learned so far. I mean, how dope is that? To get paid for talking to kids all day.

I was ready for whatever God was bringing to me and was eager to apply. I thought about how the position could be the perfect job for me and to find and fulfill my purpose. Plus, it was inside with air conditioning!

I went to sleep with the job on my mind. I applied and then I had to wait. The waiting stretched into weeks with no call from the detention center. But I was determined that if this was God's purpose for my life, I was not going to sit back and wait for the opportunity. I finally called them and explained that I turned in everything, and the secretary stated I should be receiving a call soon. This fueled my desire to dive in and get started, but I knew I had to be patient.

I finally got the call I had been so eagerly waiting for. I was excited and proud of myself for embarking on another journey. These kids were from the streets. It wasn't going to be easy because I was dealing with kids who were locked up and many who were involved in gangs. They are not angels. You have a lot of kids, all charged with something, all in the same unit for different crimes from different races, but I was still excited. I then called the security company to give them my two weeks' notice. "No more Topflight security of the world, no more flashlights, and no more sitting in a hot shack!"

On my first day of training, I woke up an hour before my alarm. I have always been taught that being at work early means you are on time. I could not wait until training began. I was thrilled to be working with the residents, which I came to learn was the name they called juveniles in the detention center.

On my first day inside the unit, they assigned me to the second floor, where the younger juvenile offenders were housed. The youngest was around 10 years old. The higher the floor, the older the kids. When I arrived, I had the biggest smile on my face. I met the crew that I would be working with and the residents in each unit. I pondered whether they would give me the booth, which is like a command center that oversees the units and seems much easier than being inside and on the floor with the kids. Just my luck, they placed me on the floor of one of the units. "It's all good, "At least I have a passion for youth. I'll be okay!" Being as cool as I am, I assumed the kids wouldn't have a problem with me and would even be comfortable talking with me. Besides, I had every pair of Michael Jordan sneakers on the market. Kids love to see people with the latest gear. The shoes make the person, according to the kids. This told the kids who I am and was a conversation starter. Kids respect you because of the type of shoes you wear, and teens love Jordan's.

I was a guy with a huge smile on my face, excited about being at work. However, the cement floors, metal tables, the uniformity of it all, and most importantly their room, made me feel emotional and sad seeing these kids being put back in their rooms like animals. Having to lock them up after a certain time or push a button to talk to the booth reinforced the concept that they could not play at a friend's house, get on the phone, or watch tv whenever they wanted. They had to ask for permission for every-thing. The reality of their isolation and circumstances was devastating to me. It was a sad picture.

As soon I stepped through the unit doors on that first day, they knew I was fresh meat. They stared me up and down to get a reaction out of me but didn't get one. After a while, I started staring back, thinking, "Why do they keep staring at me?" I guess since it was my first day, that was their way of sizing me up. I thought to myself, "I wish someone would run up… They don't know where I'm from!" My game plan was to "*act*" like I was hard. Little did they know that acting hard was a game for me. Although I had seen bad things happen to people, my life experience was nothing like what I would learn some of these kids had experienced.

A lot of people looked at those kids as if they were bad people. Unfortunately, without knowing their stories, they judged them harshly. Many of them did not have the support at home that they needed to guide them in the right direction. Some did not have significant role models or came from single-parent homes. I could understand that since my parents were divorced, and I craved my dad's attention. But the rest of my family, including my grandparents and my brother, stepped in to make sure that I hung out with the right people and gave me the skills to make good decisions. As I started in that new role, I thought I could make a difference in changing their perspective.

I took a seat alongside the other detention officer, also known as a DO, observing everyone's demeanor, facial expressions, and hand signals. I wanted to prepare myself so, I decided to head over to one of the resident's tables. I was very strategic in choosing where to sit. I tried to pinpoint the table with the residents who looked weak and wouldn't hurt a fly. I needed to get with some harm-less-looking guys so I would have no chance of being punked on my first day.

I found a table that I thought fit the bill and sat there. When I sat down, I started the conversation with a basic greeting and inquiry, "What up, fellas? What are y'all in here for?" That's right! I didn't waste any time; I went straight to the point. One kid stated he was in for robbery, another - assault with a deadly weapon, and the last one for flashing his teacher. I started thinking, I should find another table to move to; I was already a little nervous about all these guys. But I decided to stay. I also decided to share some things about my life. I wanted them to see me not as a Detention Officer but, as somebody they could talk to because I had been through similar things that they were going through.

True enough, their crimes were not comparable to some of the more severe adult crimes I had seen on the news. But flashing the teacher? That was extremely funny! So, I wanted to know more. I dove in by asking, "So what made you flash your teacher?"

The young resident then replied, "Man Chief," which is the name they used for staff, "do I *have* to bring that up?"

"I'm in here for eight hours." I replied, "It'll help make the time go by faster."

"Well, it was the end of the school year and my friends placed a bet that I wouldn't go up to my math teacher's class to harass her. She gets on everyone's nerves at school, so it was payback! On the last day, you always have that one person who is going to act a fool. Well, that one person was me this year. I jumped on my desk and pulled down my pants, simple as that."

Shocked, I asked, "Where was the teacher?"

He said, "My teacher was standing near the chalkboard. I mean, she wasn't close to me if that's what you were thinking. But she saw my underwear."

Everyone at the table started laughing. "At that time," he continued, "the teacher contacted the principle and so long story short, I ended up here. I should be out soon. I'm just waiting on my court date."

I couldn't believe my ears, but as I gazed around the entire unit, I only could imagine what the others were in for. The possibilities made me sad.

Keys to Success:

Remember, everyone has a story. Yours may be bad, but someone else's could always be worse. Reflect on the good parts of your story while using the bad parts as building blocks to a better life.

Learn from your mistakes and strive to become a better person regardless of the circumstance.

Having a positive role model, mentor, or simply someone you can talk to can really make a huge impact on your life.

MAKING A DIFFERENCE

> *"There are two types of people who will tell you that you cannot make a difference in this world: those who are afraid to try and those who are afraid you will succeed." ~ Ray Goforth - Executive director of the Society of Professional Engineering Employees in Aerospace (SPEEA) and Member of Mensa*

Everyone worked an eight-hour shift, so I knew that I would know about every juvenile in that unit if I followed my plan by the time I went home. I felt like I was locked up with them and besides, what else did I have to do? We fed them, we passed out clothes/shoes, watched while they attended school. During gym time or recreational time, we played with them. Frequently we had to break up verbal altercations. During those eight hours, if your kids got into trouble, you had to do paperwork. So, although there were many assigned tasks, there was also a lot of time for talking.

Wasn't talking part of my gift and passion anyway? Wasn't this my purpose? Well, little did I know, that was just the beginning. I loved to go around and speak with the kids about their goals. I would ask them if they thought about what their future looked like. What did they want to do when they got out of there? They would often say, "I want to finish school, play sports, or I don't know." If this was the case, I suggested they used their time to write down their goals. I wanted to give them something to think about before they got out so they would have something to look forward to. Not all kids are the same. Some loved to talk this way, while others didn't want to hear it at all.

I got to know the staff, too, who some turned out to be characters. They shared stories and lessons they learned from working in juvenile detention for so many years. Some would say, "I can't wait to retire," while others shared, "it's not the kids, but it's the people who work here." Others would have something more positive to say, like, "you can really make a difference in the kids' lives in these eight hours." Now they were speaking my language. Working at the detention center was a pivotal moment in my career. Could I really make a difference? My brain was on overdrive thinking about the possibility. If I used my time wisely while working there, it shouldn't be too challenging.

Some days, after my shift, I would sit and talk to my grandma about my day and the difference I believed I made in those youths' lives. I would explain to her the severity of some of their crimes, things that you see adults get arrested for but these children, in fact, had committed. To my emotional sharing, she always said, "Well, Boo, the only thing you can do is keep motivating them every day so they will become someone regardless of their mistakes. Pray for them and let God manage the rest." Grandma always knew the right things to say. Her words of wisdom were real and life changing. We all make mistakes and God intended for all of us to be somebody with a purpose. I knew that I could be the vehicle to help these kids follow the path that God laid out for them, and it made me even more excited to go to work every day.

I was lucky that months had gone by and no fights had happened. I had to break up a couple of verbal altercations but no fights. My crew was older than me, but they cared about me even though they had seniority. Over the years, I developed a relationship with almost every resident in the facility as I would sometimes be moved to different floors when they were short-staffed. You could move me anywhere. By watching my grandparents, I learned the importance of relationships and helping other people. I am a people person and had really earned the trust of the residents and staff. Often, I would show them my basketball tapes. I'm not going to lie; that boosted my ego a little bit because it was one of my All-star highlights when I played on TV and did very well and they would wonder why I didn't make it.

Most of the staff had at least one favorite kid they ran across, inspired, and prayed that they would make something out of themselves. My favorite kid was Craig, a young kid trapped in a grown man's body. He was 15, built like the Marvel Superhero, The Hulk, with muscles on top of muscles, and had so much respect from everybody in the building. No one, and I mean no one, wanted to mess with Craig. Sometimes when I was in the unit and Craig was upset about something, I would do whatever it took to calm him down because I knew that the crazy training they taught me wasn't going to work. I had a perfect record with no fights in my unit, and nothing was going to happen on my watch. I always tried my best to give wisdom to the kids and Craig was no different. "Craig, brother, I've known you for a long time and love you like you're my own son. I'm always violating policy by bringing you Skittles." Craig would laugh. When he would, I'd keep talking, "Your focus should be on trying to get out of here and changing your life. You have a court date in the morning, and I think they're going to let you go home. You've been in here for a long time, and we both know that whatever is bothering you is not worth it." Craig nodded and said, "You right, Mr. "Tgood," a nickname some of the staff would call me, "I got you."

I never thought I would get so attached to the kids as I did with Craig. I saw so much potential in him and I wanted to be there in the free world to witness his success story.

One morning I entered the building and received my floor assignment. I stopped by floor seven to check on Craig, who had court and was supposed to be released. I hugged him and told him I loved him and that I would see him out in the free world. Craig told me he loved me too, and as soon as I was about to leave, he asked me for some Skittles. Knowing Craig, I already had a pack in my pocket. I smiled while handing it to him. I went on to my floor feeling sad but excited for him because I knew he would do great.

This was more than just a job to me. I had developed a passion for youth and spent every day motivating them to do something great, have dreams and goals and achieve them. I was not simply there to watch over them and make sure their needs were met. I wanted to make a difference. I wanted them to know that I genuinely cared about them and their future. I would tell them things I wanted to do, like owning group homes for homeless youth and be a helping hand to anyone in need. I was all into making an impact. Although most of the juveniles there were leaving and coming right back, I knew that I was making a difference in the lives of some who we never saw again, even if I had put a bug in their ear to encourage them to want more.

However, this was still a job for me, not my career. I was still searching for a career where I could live in my purpose and follow my passion. Even though I had been there for years and I loved what I was doing, I always remember what my dad said, "Something for the resume." I didn't know what else to do. Was this what God had intended for my life? Is this my purpose? Because I have never lost my love for basketball, I questioned whether I was walking in my purpose. As much as I loved those kids, I knew I had to focus on my future and still find the purpose that God had planned for me.

Keys to Success:

We all go through obstacles in our lives, but it's the decisions you make that matter. So, choose wisely in every decision you make.

Think about the purpose that God planned for you. Are you following God's plan for your life?

What are your goals? Write down everything you want to achieve, accomplish, and receive in your life. Think about where you see yourself in five, ten, or even twenty years from now.

GOALS AND VALUES

> *"If you are willing to do more than you are paid to do, eventually you will be paid to do more than you do."*
> ~ Anonymous

In my fourth year working at the detention center, I was so proud of myself. I had touched so many lives there already that I wanted to move to a position where I could make a greater impact in the community. I didn't have a clue what that might be. I treated each kid like a human being regardless of their crime because I felt that everyone made mistakes in their lives. I am by no means perfect but had been given grace. These kids deserved the same and I planned on being there for them.

I also knew that I had been given great values from my grandparents and parents and didn't have a choice but to be great. Not everyone has the same support system that I had growing up.

My support system taught and encouraged me to set goals even if I didn't achieve all of them. That's how I operate; I set goals and work toward them. With each accomplishment, I set my sights on something new. I always write down my goals and feel a deep sense of joy as I check off each of them, understanding that some goals may take a lifetime to achieve. Even though life may get in the way of some of my goals, or they may not be within God's plan, I have vowed to never give up on any of them.

As I began to question my purpose again, I focused on bettering myself and finding a career that incorporated all my goals, desires, and vision. I knew I had nothing but time to think about it and talk to my co-workers in the unit with me about my vision. I thought again about establishing a group home for homeless kids; however, they are tough to get going, and there are many regulations for managing them. It would be quite a challenge and I wouldn't know who to call to help me. The juvenile residents loved the idea, but I also had to think about making money.

Another idea was running my own car wash and dry-cleaning business. My brain was all over the place until I decided to go back to school to get my master's degree in Counseling. I figured I couldn't lose by getting another degree that could potentially increase my pay rate. It would also make my mom even more proud of me. So that's exactly what I did. I set a new goal for myself and registered for classes. Well, you may say that this was a big jump from working as a detention officer to counseling, but honestly, that's all that I felt I was doing at the detention center anyway and enjoying it. I felt like I would be a great counselor. I had been talking to these kids on the inside and then had seen some of them in the free world, doing what I had told them. What a great feeling to see the fruits of my labor.

My new goal was set, and nothing was going to stop me. "I'm treating my education like basketball," I told myself. I was determined to earn that degree and was going to do #watevaittakes to make it happen. I also figured while I was in school, I'd have time to think about my next move. Of course, my goal was to work in a career that I would be proud of (just as much as if I were playing in the NBA) and earn a good salary

Keys to Success:

It's okay to add or change your goals.

The sky is the limit! Continue challenging yourself to accomplish more, and make it happen!

Keep in mind to utilize the advice of mentors and others who care about you to help direct your path.

STREET LIFE – A SAD REALITY

> *"If you're going down the street and you're going the wrong way, remember – God permits U-turns." ~ Suze Orman, Financial Advisor and Author*

When I arrived at work one day, I noticed some of my co-workers looking sad and talking about something. I wasn't the nosey type, but it didn't feel right to me. After I received my assignment, I asked one of the staff members, "What happened? Is everything okay?" His response broke my heart, "You remember that kid Craig that used to be on the seventh floor?"

Of course, I did. He was my boy! He had just gotten released and went back home.

He said, "Craig was killed last night."

I looked at him in disbelief, saying, "Man quit playing. Are you serious?"

Doing his best to be comforting, he said, "Yes, he was shot and killed. They said it was gang violence. I know you impacted his life, and you were one of the few of us that Craig actually listened to. You did your part."

Although I was in disbelief, I understood everything he said as I went up to my floor, still in shock. I never knew that I would feel the way I did. I felt weak and defeated. I felt like it was my fault. My mental state was not normal, and I wanted to go home. Then I thought about the others in there and I knew Craig would be looking down on me saying, "Give them some Skittles, Chief." I got my mindset back together as soon as I walked inside the unit because I didn't want any of the residents to see me as weak. Of course, those kids don't miss anything and would know right away that something was wrong. I didn't even bother going into the booth. I waved at everyone, went straight to the unit, and sat at one of the tables with the kids. I felt the only way to take my mind off things would be to keep speaking greatness in their lives, and I did.

I considered telling them what was weighing so heavily on my mind. I thought that maybe if I shared Craig's story, it could make a difference in their lives. I hoped that if I could share how much Craig meant to me and that he was killed, maybe one of them would understand the detriment of street life because they were all in gangs.

I continued to do my best to keep pouring into them with inspirational messages to hopefully change their lives when they went out in the free world. But I knew life would be difficult, especially at their age. Many of them had come from difficult households, leading them to gangs to give them the sense of community and love they craved. I knew I was doing my best to reach as many of them as possible, and I had done all that I could with Craig. Unfortunately, in there, I could only do so much. I continued to play basketball with the kids and show them all my ball-handling skills. Of course, I had to show off by giving them something to talk about back on the floor. During each shift, I sat and talked with them, still building rapport, and hopefully getting them to see that there was more to life outside than the gangs, violence, dealing, drugs, and committing crimes. I always tried to instill some positivity in them in an environment in which I had some control. I knew that many of them would go back out onto the streets, back to what they knew, and their lives were then out of my control.

Street life is a sad reality for many teens. I was doing my best to show them that there is another way. Many, not having a family support system teaching them about goals, values. and decision-making skills, could easily get pulled back into that wrong environment which got them there. Maybe they were raised by a single parent, or ultimately raised by the streets. Bad decisions start at home. Kids need a strong, solid foundation from people telling them right from wrong, about education, using themselves as an example of working hard, going to school. If parents don't talk to them about life, kids can make the wrong decisions and find themselves in juvenile detention. I wouldn't have known how to be a point guard if no one had taught me.

Family and education play important roles in the development of kids and guiding them down the right path. If teens don't have a father figure in their lives, they often look for a big brother in the streets. Mom is often the nurturer. If they don't have that, they will be out there thinking that nobody loves them. I knew that if I could help them see another way or change their attitude, they would have a better outcome on the outside.

Two years later ...

I was still wondering what I was going to do with my life a week before getting my master's degree. I started questioning myself, "What's next for me? It shouldn't be that hard anymore because I'm about to get my Master's!" Another goal in the books. Earning a master's meant I achieved more than a lot of NBA stars. Some would get drafted right out of high school and some might get drafted early from college. Some will have more money, but I had more education. "One day, I will have the money as well as two college degrees." I needed to decide, though, what job I could do to make an impact on youth. What job could I do to save people's lives? What job could I do to become a role model? What job could provide all of that and still get a decent paycheck?" I did what I knew how and went to prayer.

Keys to Success:

You can never prevent people from making their own decisions, but you can always do your best to inspire and encourage them to make better decisions.

Life can be hard at times, yet you still must follow the path that God has laid out for you.

Define what success means to you. What does it look like? Once you know what it means, do something successful for yourself and your family.

WHEN LIFE GIVES YOU LEMONS

> *"When life gives you lemons, use them to make lemonade." ~ Anonymous*

Seeing me cross the stage to accept my master's degree was another joyful time for my family. I set the bar high for my little sister, who looked up to me and was following in my footsteps. I genuinely believed that my life was a testimony not only to my sister but to the boys in the detention center. I still wanted more.

After receiving my degree, I motivated a few of the other officers to do the same. While it wasn't easy working and going to school full-time, if I could do it, my co-workers could do it too. As good as it felt to motivate my friends, it was time for me to get serious about finding another job. My dad suggested that I consider working for the police department. Since I came from a rough side of town, I thought that being a cop would mess up my relationship with friends. I wasn't involved in any criminal activities; I just knew some people who were on the wrong side of the law. There was also a stigma against cops on that side of town. Seeing people get arrested when the police are called makes you think twice about how scary that can be. On the flip side of that, and a positive note, I knew I could greatly impact the community. I took some time to think and pray about it. I listed all the positive things that could come out of being a police officer. Could I turn lemons into lemonade?

I could have a solid career (as I dreamed of) with a good salary and benefits. I could make a difference in the community and pull my friends over and scare them (only kidding). I could be a role model, and I can't forget putting the bad guys in jail. I decided to be a police officer. Finally! I was excited about my choice. The optimal thing about it was that my dad knew many of the officers, which could help me get through the process, and my friend's aunt was high up in the ranks. I was in an advantageous position to get hired. Sometimes it's all about who you know right? All I needed to do to get started was fill out the application online, and I did not waste any time doing it.

I began to envision what the future would hold for me. I wondered about the next steps, where being a police officer could take me, and the harsh reality of not living to see the future if I were killed in the line of duty. Only God knew, but I also knew God had a purpose for me. A month later, I received a call from the recruiting division of the police department. The recruiting officer explained that they would have a new cadet class in the upcoming week, and they wanted to try to get me into that class, or I would have to wait another month or so. My recruiter asked me to come in for an interview the next morning. I couldn't believe the day had come to get one step closer to my dream and my purpose.

Of course, some of the kids in the unit didn't like the fact that I was trying to become a police officer since they saw the police as a huge part of their problem. Others wanted to see me become an officer for a helping hand in situations that they might be involved in or needed some advice. My co-worker in the unit thought this was a major move, and he knew that I would be an awesome officer because of my incredible heart for people.

As I mentioned, I always try to be early, and in this case, I needed to be at the recruiting office to be prepared mentally. Mental preparation is key to how we manage the things in life that are thrown at us. I had learned through basketball how to develop mental toughness. I knew that things were not always going to go my way. I may not always win every game, and life may not go as I planned. Of course, you cannot be mentally prepared for everything that life will throw at you, but because I have always been grounded in faith, I have something to fall back on when the going got tough. That day walking into the recruiter's office was no different.

I arrived with my usual smile on my face, even though I was terrified. Throughout the interview process and even leaving the building, I kept that smile plastered on my face. I saw people staring at me. No one could know I wore that bright smile because I had faith that I would get that call-back. Three days went by, and I didn't hear from anyone. I was so frustrated and ready to put in my two weeks' notice at the detention center. I was impatient and didn't want to disappoint the kids and my co-workers. I was confident.

More days passed and still no call from the police department. I was feeling defeated and anxious. I called an officer friend of mine who reminded me, "don't worry about it, brother. You are going to drive yourself crazy. If it's meant to be, they will call you. Worrying will not make them call you faster." I felt more relaxed after the conversation with my friend and after I hung up the phone, I did just that, I went to the park and played basketball. I had to set my worries aside and trust that if it were in God's plan for me to be a police officer, everything would work out in my favor.

Every day at the detention center was a challenge. You always had to stay on your Ps and Qs because you never knew if you would have to jump in to break up a fight or if a kid felt like getting credit from his peers for hitting a DO. Imagine coming to work every day wondering how the day will be and praying that you will be okay whatever unit they put you in. As much as I loved those kids, I always had to remember it was not a daycare. Going into work while waiting on that call was an even greater challenge as I struggled to keep my composure and not let the kids see me anxious.

Suddenly, one day, I felt a vibration in my pocket and hoped it was the one call I had been waiting for. Since it was early in the morning, I knew that it had to be important. As soon as I pulled out my phone, I noticed I missed a call from the recruiter's office from the police department. I was extremely excited but forgot I was still in the unit, so I requested of my supervisor that I be relieved for a break. I contacted the recruiter as he advised that I needed to come in to go over my application to be considered for employment. The recruiter shared that to become a police officer you had to spend six months in the Academy and the good news was, we would still get paid through our training. I was all for it. Returning to the unit, nothing that could happen that day could dull that amazing feeling.

I took off work the next morning to arrive early at the police station to start the process. As I sat in my car waiting, I wondered if I was making the right decision. Was I following what God had planned for me? Was I forcing God's hand to do what I thought was best? How could a skinny dude like me arrest someone or pull someone over? Being such a nice guy, I could see it. I only got upset in basketball games. Otherwise, I was so cool and so friendly with everyone. I did think about changing my mind and going back home. Before I had the chance to pull out of the parking lot, another thought came into my head. "What about saving lives?' After hearing those thoughts, I was back on track. Was it the voice of God talking to me? Was He assuring me that this was His will? I must believe it was.

With my heart racing out of my chest, I went inside to begin the battery of interviews and tests that were to follow. They dove into my past and deep within my life. Oh my God, credit check! Surely as a recent graduate, they knew I had student loan payments. A polygraph! I had heard so much about this and had seen detective movies on TV that it seemed a bit scary. Was there some trick to pass a polygraph? A friend told me the trick was to squeeze my butt cheeks. Now I don't know what polygraph test I was taking, but I did keep a note of his wisdom.

As I sat in that chair, I felt like I was going to get electrocuted. The machine itself made me nervous. I did my best to stay calm, taking slow and deep breaths. Question after question, I thought I was good until the officer asked me if I had ever smoked weed. I responded, "No sir," I heard a different sound from the machine and quickly started squeezing my butt cheeks to see if that technique really worked, and of course, it didn't. He asked me the question again, and I replied the same way. Then he asked me to explain any involvement with weed. The only thing I could think about was in junior college when my teammates smoked weed after practice, but I never engaged in any of those extracurricular activities. I was terrified when I finally learned that I had failed the test and would have to retake it. Many thoughts were going through my mind about that last question, but I knew that God was with me and had my back no matter what.

I hate to lose, and I felt like I had lost. But God gave me another chance. They scheduled another polygraph test. I went home and prepared myself mentally for the next polygraph. This was the only thing I had left to pass. I knew that my future career was on the line. I was trying to do better, but it was so challenging.

I returned the next day to do the polygraph over again. This time I was cool, calm, and collected taking deep breaths. Before the questions started rolling in, the new officer was cool and told me just to nod my head either yes or no to each question. It helped make my nervous system calm down a bit and suddenly, boom! I was done before you know it, and I didn't even have to squeeze my butt cheeks this time! I had passed the test and after everything was processed, I was hired and part of academy class number 209. I eagerly shook the officer's hand and vowed to become one of the best police officers.

When I went back to work, I immediately told my supervisor that I would be putting in my notice to leave because I would be working for the Houston Police Department. My co-workers and the staff were excited for me. Many of the kids were upset that I was leaving and many were upset that I would be the "law." I promised the kids that I would see them in the free. I truly meant I would be there for them no matter what. I learned so much from them; I felt like I was leaving family. Many people there meant so much to me and I knew that the experience I had gained would carry over into this next stage of my life. As difficult as it was to say goodbye, the career I prayed about was at hand.

Keys to Success:

When life throws you lemons, YOU must decide to make something out of it. Whether sweet or bitter lemonade, you get to decide.

Mental toughness is required in life to handle the ups and downs that are inevitably going to come. What will you do to develop mental toughness?

Never forget that your background record, positive or negative, can make a difference for your future.

FINDING MY PURPOSE

> *"Stop chasing the money and start chasing the passion." ~ Tony Hsieh – Internet Entrepreneur and Venture Capitalist*

I went from wearing a peach fuzz mustache and chin hair to having to cut everything off, leaving me looking like the R&B singer Babyface as I began this journey at the police academy. It was time to put in the work, study hard, get serious about life. The physical skill part of the training was the easiest for me. I had never shot a gun before, so that was a challenge. But I faced it head-on. There were over 60 people in our class and since I was so competitive, being number one meant a lot to me. My mind was set on the physical fitness part. I had a great support system at home that helped me practice my cadences because it was horrible. I even tripped over my own foot while we were in action. Still, I wasn't going to let anything stop me from. accomplishing my mission.

Months went by. Academically I was in good standing, but I still had a lot of work to do. I was on academic probation twice and I knew I had to study extra hard, to bring my test scores up. My favorite skills test, which was the physical fitness part, included a mile and a half run, push-ups, sit-ups, and the 300-meter run. I heard about people from previous cadet classes breaking records; it was my turn! After doing great in the other drills, it was time for the big one, the mile and a half. Although I had been more of a sprinter than a long-distance runner, I was as up for the challenge, even with the nervous butterflies in my stomach.

As we were on the line to start, I kept talking to myself, giving myself encouragement to control my breathing and maintain a good pace. This was my time to show off. This was record-breaking time. As we took off, I knew I was doing great, until I wasn't. My oxygen was fading, and I couldn't keep up the pace. No matter how much I motivated myself, I couldn't go any faster. But I was still ahead of the pack. As I was about to approach the finish line on the last lap, I gave it all I had. My legs felt like noodles and it didn't seem like my soul was in my body anymore. I was done. I always put 100% into everything I did and would not let something like exhaustion stop me. I then went back on the track to help others who were struggling with a little motivation. Still playing the point guard role like I did in basketball; it was in my nature to always check on my teammates and help them.

Even though I didn't break the record, I came in first place with a grade of 100 percent. Motivation Tip: Whatever you want to do in life, speak it into existence. That's exactly what I did. Next, I had to pass the shooting test. I hate to admit it, but I sucked at shooting. The trainer yelled at me so much that I had a nightmare of him saying slowly, "squeeze the trigger." I was that bad and I was in tears a couple of times. Trying to act hard to stay mentally tough did nothing. I was scared. This was the longest skills test of my life. I even had to cheat a little bit by going to the gun range. What was I supposed to do when dry firing (practicing discharging the firearm without ammunition) at home every day wasn't doing anything for me? I had to shoot the gun. Our instructors would also tell us to put a penny on top of our weapon to practice our trigger pull at home, with an unloaded gun of course. If the penny falls off the weapon, that means you're not in control of it. The penny fell off my weapon all the time. Although it seems like it took forever, I finally passed the shooting test. I never prayed so much in my life until I went through that torture. But they say God answers prayers and He sure did answer mine. At one point, I thought I would lose my job because I couldn't hit a target. As a police officer, this is an important skill to have.

Keys to Success:

Just like I have control of my weapon, you have control of your destiny.

There is power in the words that we speak, so be sure to speak life into existence.

No one is going to hand you anything. You must work hard and earn it.

SCARED TO DEATH

> *"For life and death are one, even as the river and the sea are one." ~ Kahlil Gibran – Lebanese-American Writer, Poet, and Visual Artist*

B ack in the classroom, I could almost see the light at the end of the tunnel. The last thing to do before graduation was to get tased. YES! We were really getting tased! If I had known that getting tased was part of the process, I promise I wouldn't have joined, but it was too late. Y'all should know by now that I am NOT the quitting type. I had not given up on anything yet, so why would I start? I couldn't understand why we had to get tased. The instructors explained we would be tased to understand how it would feel if we used it against someone else. For example, if we had to go to court and someone asked if we know how it felt to be tased, we could accurately describe it. Before we started, the instructors gave us two options; either we could do it on our own where the person stands up and the instructor shoots the dart into their back, or with a partner as two people sit down and they place the wires on their shoes. How about not do it at all? Why wasn't that an option? I made some friends in class and one of them was a woman I used to help during the skills process. She messed up a lot. You think my shooting was bad! I didn't think this was the job for her, but at least she wasn't scared. She asked if I would like to get tased with her and I smiled; you couldn't say no to her. She seemed confident while I was really scared.

When the day came, they told everyone to meet in the gym. Some people seemed excited about it; some people seemed a bit nervous, and some people, like me, had wanted to call in that day. They gave us instructions on the type of taser to be used and demonstrated the safety measures. It was game time as everyone started lining up. The first person to go was a classmate. As soon as the instructors said, "Taser, Taser," you heard a pop and then a scream! "Ahhhhhhh!!!" After five seconds of watching my classmate get tased, shaking, and screaming as they guided him down to the ground, it was time for me to go home. I walked to the back of the line. This was a life and death situation, not physically but for my dreams and ambitions.

They were not making this any easier on my mental health. My partner stood by my side and asked, "You ready to go?" It should have been me asking her that, implying that we should GO – like right out the door! Instead, I responded that I was ready. Let's just get this crap out the way. Since we were doing it as partners, our being tased situation was a little bit different, and it made me feel ten times better, but I was still nervous. As we looked at each other and walked toward the instructors, they told us to sit down on the ground. This was going to be interesting. Were they going to shoot the taser at us while we are sitting down? I must've asked the question aloud, because one of the instructors responded, "No, we're going to clamp the wires to the side of your boots." We were the first people in the class to go together as partners, majority of the class went by themselves, so I couldn't prep myself. All I could think about was trying not to urinate on myself.

The instructor continued giving us instructions, but all I saw were his lips moving. Everything was quiet and seemed to be going in slow motion. My partner looked at me with a sweet smile as always, and I looked back at her with an expression of "get me out of here." The instructor yelled "Taser, Taser" and pulled the trigger. The electric shock went through our boots, all the way through our body and suddenly, we both flew back on the mat screaming and couldn't stop. After five seconds, it stopped. We were done. While sticking out my chest, I told everyone, "that was it? That wasn't anything. Who is going next?" Oh boy, how I played it off well. Now that it was over, I could go back to my normal self, motivating everyone to get through this pain and suffering. Thank God everyone got through it, and no one had to go to the hospital.

Completing Field Problems was the last test in the process. Field Problems was everything we learned in the academy. I can't forget about the fun part of us fighting the instructors in the ring after running through a whole obstacle course. Which was good because no matter how exhausted you are in the real world; you have to stay in the fight, or you could possibly lose your life if you give up. Field problems shouldn't be too hard for me. This last test was a determining one; you could pass or get fired. During that long stressful process, I made some mistakes, but I passed. My friend, who was my partner when I got tased, didn't make it. She had the right attitude and smile. She had the heart for the job and as her journey at the academy ended, my heart went out to her.

In my own journey at the police academy, I learned so many things. I had a better understanding of what was required as a police officer. I was going to face battles every day that could threaten my life. I had to be prepared mentally and physically. I had to be quick on my feet and my mind always had to be sharp. The taser situation was just one example of being scared to death; I knew that there was more to come.

Keys to Success:

Sometimes when you try to achieve a goal, barriers will come to derail you from your goals and your vision. Be prepared to break down any barrier that comes between you and your destiny.

You are a leader not a follower. Never back away from something that you really want in life.

Even though things might seem dark at the beginning, there is always light at the end of the tunnel. STAY FOCUSED!

ANOTHER GRADUATION!

> *"Your education is a dress rehearsal for a life that is yours to lead."* ~ *Nora Ephron – Journalist, Writer, and Filmmaker*

First school and now the police academy. I could not believe that I had reached another goal, another milestone in my life. It felt so good knowing that I had set my mind to it and now it was happening. I looked sharper than a thumbtack from my shiny boots up to my clip-on tie. The academy graduation was the bomb! It seemed like every police officer in the city was there, as were the chief and the mayor. I was so nervous and excited.

The announcer moderating the ceremony read, "The top performer for Skills in Physical Training with 100 percent, Sheldon Theragood!" My friends and family were so excited! I didn't trip or fall on my way to the stage. Of course, I had a huge smile as everyone took pictures with me. I was now the real "popo" (law enforcement). I gave the award I received to my Grandma for teaching how to pray about things and not to worry." Clear Lake Police Station was the station I picked to train at, and within days of graduation, I reported for duty.

One year later ...

I had to train on all three shifts: night, day, and morning and with different trainers per shift. My first trainer drove me nuts, and honestly terrified me. I think he was trying to fail me. I was working hard to learn officer safety because I knew that it could save my life. Yet, I was terrible at using the key map to locate a call, but eventually, I made it through his obstacle course.

I thought working the evening shift would be better. The night shift was the devil if you were not used to it. My trainer made the evening shift more relaxed for me because of how he trained, although this shift was very busy. He was relaxed and cool, told me to take my time, guided me through all the calls that needed police in our area. We had so many calls on the board that it almost made me want to go back to the night shift. Night shift calls were slow. It was like everyone was asleep and not breaking laws at that time. During the evening shift, you had all types of calls to choose from 911 hang-up calls, accidents, disturbances, traffic hazards. You name it. Taking as many calls as I could helped me get prepared for evaluation. At Clear Lake, we might not have had the calls some stations had, but it provided good training.

My morning shift trainer was old school and had 30 plus years on me. I knew he was going to make sure that I did everything right according to our policy and procedures. The morning calls weren't as heavy as the evening, but at a certain hour, it would get busy. One afternoon I got a call that I never had before - a welfare check. This type of call is when a concerned citizen, workplace, family member, or friend contacts the police to check on someone who has not been heard from or seen for an unusual amount of time or out of their normal behavior. A family member, the complainant's cousin, stated that she had spoken with him the day before and he was feeling depressed and suicidal. My partner asked if she could show us where he lived. As soon as we got to the door, the property's maintenance person was there to let us in. I was hoping nothing had happened to him. My heart was racing as we approached.

We beat on the door, yelling his name to see if he would open it. Several more knocks, but still no answer. At that point, we went inside and called his name once again, still no answer. As we entered the apartment, we saw clothes and furniture all neatly put together. We then slowly entered one of the bedrooms. My trainer went in first as I waited for him to let me know when to come in. As soon as I walked in, I stopped in my tracks in shock, not believing what I saw. I wanted to walk back out of the apartment. The walls were covered in red like a horror movie. All I kept thinking was, is this for real? This was my first suicide call. My trainer must have seen hundreds of these cases since he walked in like it was nothing. He kept calling me to come to look; I had no choice. This man could not deal with life anymore and used a shotgun to kill himself.

A series of questions started to flow through my mind. I wondered what this person had been through that was so horrible that he needed to do this. Where was his help? Did he even want help? How long had this been going on? Mental health is nothing to play with and your life is so valuable. If you have a mental illness, please seek a therapist, a close friend, anyone you can trust and talk to. Trust me when I say that I've been through deep depression myself, but I had the support to help me through it. That is why I am still here to tell a story. Remember that someone cares about you and loves you dearly, and your life is worth living. It made me so sad to know that this guy resorted to taking his life when he could have gotten the help he needed.

I had to go outside and tell a concerned family member that her cousin was deceased. As soon as I approached, she knew that something was wrong and began to cry. I then got nervous and didn't say anything, "Come on, Sheldon, you got this, bro." This was my first time. "Imagine this as the basketball game and your team needs you. I finally started to speak and told her that her cousin was there, and she hugged me. I really didn't have to say anything else because she already knew from the way I was moving and tried to console her. I gathered all her information as we waited for the medical examiner to arrive. I still couldn't believe that I had experienced this horrible event and knew it was going home with me.

Now I had to write my report, which had to be detailed. I didn't complain at all, practice does make perfect. While typing my report, my trainer told me that I did a wonderful job speaking with the family member because that could be tough for some people, and he was proud of me.

I passed my evaluation and appreciated all three of the guys for helping me through the process. I learned that everyone polices differently; my night shift trainer was stricter but assured me that superior officers wanted to make sure I made it home safe at the end of the day. My evening shift trainer was more relaxed and cooler but still got the job done. My morning old school trainer made sure my "i's" were dotted and my "t's" were crossed figuratively speaking and made sure I knew the law. They all were awesome, and I knew that I was going to take a skill from each trainer to prepare me for evaluation, which I passed. I even did well at key mapping, which was my weakest skill.

While Clearlake was my training station, I picked Northeast Patrol as my permanent station. Northeast carried the nickname "The Rock" based on the criminal activity it managed. Just as I used to look at my basketball uniform knowing that I would put in my best effort, I thought to myself, "When I put on this uniform, I'm going to be the best I can be and give it all I got." I envisioned myself making a significant impact on the city of Houston, being a role model, a friend, a mentor, someone you could talk to about any situation, an all-around awesome person. Instead of running from me, I wanted citizens to know that they could run to me, knowing that I could help. I knew that was going to take time because so many people were afraid of police officers. In my head, as a young, cool-as-ice rookie, I knew I could help change that. Now, if you break the law, I suggest you not run to me, but run to the jail and turn yourself in because I still must do my job. But helping you to become a better person? I'm all in. At least that was my goal.

I love helping people as I did at the juvenile detention center. I love to see people happy and feeling like that they can conquer the world. I was a bit nervous starting at my new station, but God is a great and always has my back, so I knew I was going to be fine.

Keys to Success:

Your life is valuable!! Know and believe how important you are, and others will then recognize your value.

When you wake up every morning, remind yourself to give your best every day.

Take the notes you took from your mentors and apply them to your own life.

A DAY IN THE LIFE OF
A POLICE OFFICER

> *"Blessed are the peacekeepers: for they shall be called the children of God." ~ Matthew 5:9 (KJV)*

I couldn't sleep. Training was over and it was a new day. Time to put some sterling silver shine on my badge and baby oil on my boots. Building a relationship on my new beat as a rookie started with making a good impression. When I arrived at my new station, I saw some of my former classmates and, man, we were so excited to see each other and ready to be police officers. I patiently waited through roll call to hear if I was being assigned a partner. One of my classmates from the academy was partnered with me. He is my homeboy and a great guy. He was not scared of anything and looked like a pit bull because of all his muscles. He is a beast. As we got into the patrol car to respond to a disturbance call, and he slid behind the wheel, a scene from the "Bad Boys" movie kept playing through my head. As he was flying through the streets, scaring me, he had me thinking that we were dispatched to an emergency call with lights and sirens. The faster he drove, the more I held on to the arm rest and pressed my foot on the floorboard like I had brakes on my side.

I thought, "if we run into something, I'll be prepared to scream before it happens." I was more scared in the car than I was on the streets. He was the intimidating one and I was the skinny, toothpick-looking guy who always had a Kool-Aid smile. I made people more relaxed and comfortable with my demeanor, but I was still always ready for action.

I learned a lot in that one day, seeing what people go through in their everyday lives. I was thinking to myself, "are there going to ever be calls when people just say, 'Thank you for your service, and here are some gifts to show how much we appreciate you'?" Of course not, I doubt if people ever do that. The calls on our board ranged from domestic disturbances to assaults in progress and shootings. I didn't have training for some of these calls. That's the thing about being a police officer, there is no way to train you for every call you might take. Sometimes you must use common sense and make it back home. The things that you see and that are happening around you as a police officer will make you question whether you will make it back home at the end of the day. It will make you pause to tell your family you love them before you leave the house because it might be the last time that you talk to them. You learn to appreciate life seeing what we see every day.

After a period of partnering with other officers, it was finally time to ride by myself. I was excited but wondered what would happen if I got into something. Without a partner I would have to use my radio, and I hate being on the radio because everybody is listening and if you make a mistake everyone hears it. Maybe you are talking too much or saying the wrong thing or being long-winded or not using the right terminology. The radio drove me crazy.

After getting our assignments one day, I discovered a former classmate was riding solo too. The cool thing about that was we were in the same beat so we could have each other's back. Knowing that made being on my own much easier and less stressful. I also didn't have to worry about anyone's driving or being late for a call. Sometimes I even thought about going into neighborhoods where there are many young folks and jam the music on my loudspeaker. I bet they would be dancing and seeing how cool the police could be. Even though I wanted to, I had to remember that I was a rookie, and my bright idea would make it easier to get fired. You might as well call me Axel Foley (the Eddie Murphy character from the Beverly Hills Cop movie franchise). I was hoping I didn't have to chase anybody.

As I checked the board, I noticed a call that said, "welfare check." The last time I did a welfare check was a bit much. This situation was a little different. I was to check on an older person whose family couldn't get in touch with him for days. I thought to myself, "Hey, this shouldn't be bad at all." I took the call, put the address in my GPS, and got to the location as soon as possible. As soon as I pulled up, the person's granddaughter was standing in the driveway and gave me the details about her elderly grandfather. All I kept thinking was that he probably died in the house from old age. I called for back-up and when the other officer arrived, we made our way to the door. I don't know why but I was extremely nervous. As the granddaughter unlocked the front door, we began to call out his name.

"Clifford!!" The smell inside the house was horrible. As we made our way to a bedroom, we noticed the door was open and there we saw Mr. Clifford lying on his bed with nothing but underwear on. As we approached the bed, the smell got worse. He had passed away. I had the tough task of telling his granddaughter, but I had developed the skill of speaking with distressed folks from a comparable situation in Clear Lake.

When she saw my face, she shook her head. She already knew. Tears flowed from her eyes. For a moment, I hoped in reflection, that I have people who would care about me enough to check up on me daily in my older years. You don't know how much that means.

When I left the scene that day, I started thinking about the work I was doing and questioned if it was something I planned on doing for the rest of my life. I'm the type of person who tries to be ahead of the game, always think-ing about what's next. What is God's plan for me? I really wish I could see it. Who would have thought that I would become a police officer?

The next day I was back at it again. I took a lot of pride in my job and I was always happy, and people made me even happier. If I didn't smile, then someone would have thought something was wrong with me. Every day it was the same thing; roll call, assignments, and back on the streets we go. As rookies, we always got the worst car, but my positive thoughts told me that it could have been worse. Being a police officer is not as bad as I thought it was. Everyone is so cool, and it makes my day even more amazing.

I got to know all the store managers at every store in my beat. I know the importance of building positive relationships and sharing positive vibes. If I wanted to bring that powerful love to the community, I had to get to know everybody and build those relationships. You might as well call me "Officer Friendly."

One afternoon, I heard loud rings from my radio, meaning a code one call in progress. I get nervous every time I hear that, and I pray the dispatcher doesn't call my unit number. After the second loud sound, the dispatcher called out another unit's number and then added "shooting in progress." My heart sank! I drove with my heart racing. I was able to get to the neighborhood quickly. The dispatcher's voice came through the radio again that it was a confirmed shooting and that one male had been shot. My whole demeanor changed now.

As I got near the shooting scene, I saw so many people hanging out on the other side of the street from where the shooting happened. I thought maybe they had been having a block party or something. I am from the hood, so my common sense kicked in and, in most neighborhoods, you would have all the family members living in the same area; Uncle Jimmy Ray and Brother Tommy would be staying next door to each other, Cousin Earl and Aunt Pearl would be across the street, and Grandma Louis and Papa Joe would be on the next street over. People were yelling and crying. I ran into one of my coworkers on the scene and asked what happened. Before he could say anything, I saw a person being detained and placed in the police vehicle's back seat. "You see the guy that they're putting in the back of the police vehicle? He allegedly shot another person three times over a situation involving a female. I didn't get all the details, but as of right now, that's what we've been told from one of the family members. They were both teenagers, from my understanding. The other teen is deceased in the backyard."

I was shocked. A teenager was shot and killed. Are you serious? This was my first murder scene, but it was also my first scene involving a teenager. This is something that I never thought I would see happen. At the juvenile detention center, I would hear kids talk about things they saw on the streets. Of course, I saw it on the news, but I hoped I would never have to see it in person. I was in shock. Reality hit because these kids were just kids and now his life and future had been taken from him.

While I'm in my own world staring at what's going on around me, I heard someone say, "Officer Theragood!" One of the Sergeants at the scene asked me to go to the back and secure the teen's body. Now mind you, I don't know what securing the body means, so thank God he elaborated. I had to make sure no one went into the backyard to get near the body. I had to remember how hood people can get when a loved one gets killed. It can be total chaos. I slowly walked toward the backyard. As I was walking, I saw clothes on the ground before seeing where the teen was laying. From the looks of it, they were fighting, and things were scattered everywhere. I finally saw what I thought and hoped I would never have to see in my whole police career, the dead body of a teenager.

I was terrified, nervous, emotionally depressed; my heart was heavy. I totally went flashback mode from the juvenile detention center remembering all those kids and hearing all their stories, the crimes they committed, and the things they had seen. I would motivate them to change their lives and do whatever it takes to be someone before something happens and they end up dead. Looking at this body laying lifeless on the ground, I couldn't help but think that this could be one of those kids I talked to. Although I knew they listened to me on the inside, when they leave and go back to the free world where all their friends, bad environment, and toxic people get back in their circle, all those things wouldn't matter anymore. While standing by the body, I remembered my grandma telling me never to question God. But at that moment, I needed to know why. Sometimes I wish I could have made it in time for the bullet to hit me instead of the kid. This kid could have had all types of dreams. I know you have angels up there that could have stopped this from happening. This is not cool. This hit home hard. There were many officers there, but I was chosen to go to the backyard to secure that area – I was the one! It could have been ANYONE. He could have told me to do anything, take statements, transport the suspect. Out of all the officers, he told me to go back there where the kid was. Why me?

A question came to my mind. Was God sending me a message? I heard the question clearly, "what are you going to do about it?" While looking up at the sky, I repeated, "What am I going to do about it?" Y'all might think I had lost my mind, but I could hear myself spiritually. You must build that real deep relationship with God to know what I'm talking about. I'm not about to start preaching, but this felt like a setup for me to understand that God was using me. I was the chosen one to go out and help prevent these things from happening. I asked God about angels that could have helped in this situation, but I realized that I am that angel. I knew right then and there that God chose me to go out and save youths' lives. This whole situation seemed like it was planned out for me to make a difference. It seemed like God planned it out. From working at the juvenile detention center mentoring kids for years, to becoming a cop, to the Sargent telling me to secure the teenager's body, if I'm the chosen one from God, then I'm ready to make Him proud and go to work. I know that

God has plans for everyone's life, even that young man who lost his that day.

Keys to Success:

Pick and choose your battles. They're not worth losing your life over.

Things may happen that are beyond your control at times. Stay positive and respond to the situation as best as you can.

Take pride in everything you work hard for, regardless of the task.

THE MASTER'S PLAN

> *"For I can do everything through Christ, who gives me strength." ~ Philippians 4:13 (NLT)*

I f God is for me, who can be against me? After that day, my brain was on overdrive. I knew I had a lot of ideas about what I wanted to do with youth, but I realized I needed to build relationships with the kids to guide them in the right direction like a mentor. How about I become a mentor? It's a start. I immediately thought about starting with family first. Most people I know have some unruly kids in their family that they wish they could help guide in the right direction. I thought, "I'll just put the word out and see what happens." I spent the rest of the day with this on my mind. I went to sleep with this on my mind. I became hyper-focused on helping save kids like the one I had seen laying in the grass. That really messed me up mentally, but I knew I had work to do, and God had my back. How could I do one-on-one mentoring, make it fun, and have teens still learn something at the same time?

I woke up feeling like I never slept at all, but like my grandma always said, "don't forget to say your prayers." I began to ask God for help as soon as I opened my eyes. "God, I need your help at this moment. What can I do to make an impact on these kids' lives to help prevent all this violence?" I started my day off as usual, at the gym, but then I drove around thinking of God's master plan. What could it be that God wants me to do? My heart, mind, and emotions were spinning. How about I step out on faith and host an event, speaking to teens about real situations, awareness of violence, giving them hope that they can make it regardless of the past mistakes they've made? I questioned God. "But, God, you know good and well I am not a public speaker at all." This was a barrier that I had to break through. I would do what God had laid out for me to do by any means necessary. A plan began to form. I would speak to the kids for at thirty minutes dressed in uniform and give them free school supplies afterward. I would post something on social media and see how it would go. I decided to call the mentoring initiative "Real Talk with Youth and Back to School Supply Giveaway." Even if one person showed, I would do my best to give that one kid all I got to be encouraged and ready to do better.

Ain't nothing to it but to do it. I decided to have it downtown at one of Houston's most popular recreation centers where the NBA greats play their summer leagues.

I was so pumped up and ready and nervous at the same time. Then it hit me! How was I supposed to pay for the school supplies that God put in my heart to give and promised on the social media flyer I had created? A little naïve, I figured I would pay for them out of my own pocket and set a budget of $50. Long story short, I had no idea how many people were coming or what to expect. What if I had more than, say, ten people? I couldn't believe I was really doing this! Following my heart and God's path was awesome, but man, it required so much planning and money, but whatever it takes to save the youth, right? This is what I was asking for.

You could say I am not the type to brag about things I was doing but I like to get it done. I didn't even tell my mom that I was doing this event. I know that in different neighborhoods, people don't really like cops, but I wanted to be that one cop who could change that conversation. The streets were so busy sometimes it was hard to even take a break, let alone build those relationships. How was I going to do what God called me to do if I was stuck doing these calls all the time? I was mentally exhausted from all the conversations going on in my head. Yet, I had confirmations that 15 people were bringing their teens to my upcoming event! My heart started pounding like a basketball. I knew that God was working.

The day of the event arrived, and I was so nervous I could hardly breathe. I pulled out a fresh uniform, gathered all the supplies, and headed out early. It was game time. Although it was just fifteen kids expected to arrive, I prayed to have the whole recreation center someday filled. Nothing wrong with speaking my dreams into existence.

I started to panic. What if no one shows up? What if they are bored? I'll start by telling them about myself, my basketball days, which always gets the kids excited. Remember my goals. I need to share my experiences of being a police officer and let them know how valuable their lives are. God, you are awesome and always on time! I had been working toward this very moment my entire life and didn't even know it. It was time to put the shy me aside and step out and become the person that God had planned for me to be since I was born.

As my guests came in and found their seats, I realized that my vision was happening right before my eyes. I was amazed. Everything went as planned and I spoke well. I made eye contact with everyone and the audience was engaged. I felt like I had scratched the surface of making change and developing a relationship with these young people and their families. To top it off, I had enough school supplies for every kid. I'm always thinking about something bigger and even as I finished this first event, I was thinking about how many more kids I could serve in the future.

Everyone can do whatever they want to do, but I didn't just aim for the stars. I wanted to reach the moon and I hoped to encourage others to do the same. You can achieve anything that you set your mind to. Why couldn't I do this with students in schools? Who doesn't want a down to earth cop to impact their students at their schools? I added the pictures from the day's event on my social media and immediately started getting people sending me messages that they wanted me to come and speak at their school. Did they know what was on my heart? Sometimes you must watch what you say or even think because it might just come into existence. In my case, that is exactly what happened. I knew that this was God's Master Plan for my life, and He was going to make it all fall into place if this was His will.

Keys to Success:

God has a Master Plan for your life. It's up to you to find out what it is.

You must step out of your comfort zone to make changes for the best.

Speak your dreams out into the universe to help them come into existence.

WALK IN YOUR PURPOSE

> *"It's not enough to have lived. We should be determined to live for something."* ~ Winston S. Churchill
> – Prime Minister of the United Kingdom (1940 – 1945)

I still wanted to do more, and I needed to think hard on this. What else could I do in the community to change the lives of young people? With all the things that God has done for me so far, I was sure I had nothing to worry about. Although these extra events at schools would make juggling my work schedule difficult, I was willing to do anything to save a kid's life. I had stepped out in faith to do what I prayed to God to do and look at how He is using me. God has a plan for everyone's life, and He will give you the dreams and the skills to achieve remarkable things. Everyone has the potential to do great things.

I was transferred to another station, taken off the beat; and assigned to transporting prisoners. This was another blessing since it gave me more exposure to another aspect of the justice system and gave me more time to think about my next event. I wanted to get more engaged with the community. I felt that not only did the youth need a great message, but they needed to be engaged with others in giving.

In this new position, I met some great people with seniority who taught me so much about the job and life in general. If you're trying to encourage me to be great, my ears are open to listening. Through all the negative that you hear from people and their personal lives, it's always good to hear something positive. It would be awesome if everyone could encourage each other or compliment them on the excellent job they have done. But you know life is not that easy or rosy!

One day I was doing my job transporting prisoners when I saw someone I knew. "Is that who I think it is?" Of all people, I wouldn't think this guy, a former friend, an All-American basketball player in high school who went off to play for a Division One college, would be coming to the county jail. Seeing people go to jail for whatever reason was sad to me but seeing your own friend or someone you know just tears you apart. Everyone makes mistakes and bad decisions at some point in their lives. Seeing my old friend made me think even more about life, my 'what if" factor, and how I could have been just like my friend. But God had bigger plans for my life which included staying on the right side of the law. It broke my heart to see my friend there and gave me even more motivation to do what I was doing and to walk in the purpose that God was starting to reveal to me.

When I went to my first school to speak with the students, the teacher asked me to speak about gun violence. Now I am the first to say that I am no expert in this area, but I would give it my best as I do with everything. I was excited and determined to at least act like I knew what I was doing. If this was part of my purpose, then I was going to walk confidently in whatever God had planned for me.

Walking into the school, I suddenly got nervous again. Why? I was just following God's path. What should I be nervous about? He has never left me before. When I walked into the classroom, all the kids were clapping and yelling. I was about to do the same thing because I thought someone important was walking in behind me, but no one was there. They were clapping for me. Thinking to myself, *Wow, that teacher must have told them to show me some love because I honestly didn't do anything to deserve the warm welcome they gave me.* This greeting helped to boost my spirit and my confidence, and I hadn't even spoken yet. I began to act like I knew what I was doing, and boy, did that get the kids' attention. I spoke about my life experiences and being a police officer, and of course, the kid who got murdered. I had to be real. If you really want to save a life, you can't cut any corners but bring it right to them. That's what I did. After I was finished, you don't have to be a rocket scientist to know what kind of questions these fifth graders asked me as a police officer. "Have you used your gun before? Have you arrested anyone? Have you seen a dead body? Why did you become an officer?" As they shook my hand and waved goodbye, they called me the "cool" police officer. By the time I left, they all wanted to be police officers when they grow up.

Keys to Success:

Everyone has the potential to be great and do remarkable things. Make a list of the powerful things you want to achieve in life.

We ALL make mistakes, but it's not the end of the road. Be sure you learn the lesson in every mistake you make.

Always be prepared and ready for new opportunities that are headed your way!

A BIGGER IMPACT

> *"The only limit to your impact is your imagination and commitment."* ~ Tony Robbins – Author, Coach, Speaker, and Philanthropist

This was beginning to be a routine thing. The word got around, and I was the officer to call on to speak to their students for every career day. While speaking at schools and mentoring the youth was awesome, there had to be more. I meditated and prayed to God for vision to help me do something different, and in deep thought, I remembered my grandma saying, "Boo, it's better to give than to receive." That was it. My grandma's words had done it again. I felt the need to have a team of youth who could go out with me and serve struggling families, homeless people, folks who couldn't do for themselves, and do just what my grandma said, "give back." The whole point would be for youth to experience serving others, learning about people who made bad decisions in their lives, and seeing how tough it can be. I wanted to give teens an opportunity to learn how not to take life for granted and treat others with respect.

God had given me this vision, but now I needed to figure out how to make it happen, and my vision needed a name. What better way to express what I was born to do than by using my own name to do it! Theragood Deeds, Incorporated, a non-profit organization, was born! God is always on time and amazes me every single time.

Sometimes I wish I could go back to the detention center and get 50 of those kids to bring with me and impact the whole city. This is still a wish, and nothing is going to change my thoughts on this. One day I'll somehow make it work. When I was working in the detention center, most of those kids who were in there committed a violent crime. This outreach team could be powerful as it would allow them to learn about homeless people and their situations, experience folks who are struggling, kids and adults who can't do for themselves, and other youth suffering from permanent medical conditions. Our outreach team would focus on impacting all these groups of people's lives through giving. My goal is to turn hate into love. Through Theragood Deeds, I wanted to create the perfect team of youth to impact the world one good deed at a time. I was totally committed to walking in God's path, although I knew it would be quite a challenge. But I'm the chosen one, right?

I had a vision mapped out on what I wanted to do to impact our youth. It didn't matter where they come from, whether they were at-risk kids or straight-A students, I wanted them all to be part of my team. I wanted to inspire teens to become successful individuals within their personal lives, families, and communities. I hoped to give them a new perspective on life versus only what they saw all around them. God gave me the vision to teach young people how to be cheerful givers to less fortunate people. I was so excited to see these ideas flowing from my brain. Now I just had to figure out a way to put a youth team together.

I loved working in the jail because it gave me so much time to figure out how to get this team started. I was doing the best I could to guide kids in the right direction while God was using me and giving me this opportunity. I was very impatient, though. I wanted this wish of creating a non-profit to come true immediately. But I had to understand that it's all in God's timing. In my head and my prayers, I kept saying, "God, please hurry." I knew that His plan for my life was going to give kids a head start in life. When I was growing up, I participated in the youth program at my church. I think this is where my interest in giving back to others was sparked as well as from my grandmothers' efforts. But I wanted kids to get all the insight from these awesome people as quickly as possible. I felt as if the faster I could get started, the more kids I could save.

Like in sports, you play to win; in the community, we play to save lives. I am so humbled by everything that God has given me in my life, and I try my best to thank Him for even the trivial things I am blessed with. I am grateful for Him waking me up in the morning, giving me health and strength to go out and impact someone's life. If you don't do it already, I encourage you to be thankful for whatever you have, even if what you have does not seem that great.

I started my community service project by taking some of the teens to visit two of my homeless buddies who lived underneath the bridge. They shared their stories and explained how their poor decisions and mistakes landed them in their current situations. They made me think about my own life and the decisions that I had made and how my life could easily have turned out differently. They admitted that they didn't have a mentor to guide them back on track or someone who really cared as I did for these kids. Although this first act taught us so many lessons, I learned while working with kids in the detention center that this wasn't a cure for their behavior. I expected mistakes to be made by these guys in the future, but at least it gave them something to think about and they couldn't say that no one ever told them.

A week later, one of my former coworkers, a good friend of mine who had so much passion for the youth, contacted me and told me he knew someone who was like a mom to all these kids at a local park and told me it would be a great partnership if we teamed up. I reached out and told her my vision and she was willing to help and get her kids involved. I knew this was going to work out well by the way she spoke about her group. I could tell that she had a lot of love for the youth. I knew this was all just a piece of a huge puzzle that God had planned for me. Sometimes, as hard as it seems, you must sit still and let God do His thing.

This is what I've been waiting for. I had a solid relationship with the soup kitchen downtown, and I arranged for some of the kids to help. I could already envision nothing but good vibes before this event got started. Some youths have never had the opportunity to give back or hear those words that we all crave, "you are doing a great job." I wanted these kids to know and understand how important they are. I was so ready to get this thing started. As I laid out money from my own pocket to buy toiletries for the homeless, I questioned God like I always do. Sometimes I make myself laugh being silly when I know God is like, "I got you." He always does!

Theragood Deeds, Inc. was on the way. This is what I'd been praying for and look at God. Our event was scheduled for Loaves and Fishes Soup Kitchen downtown, and all I had to do was announce on social media to share our event so we could have more youth come out to volunteer and do something great in the community. Now, you know, I always think big - imagine if 100 kids gave their hearts out to the homeless.

I don't watch the news because it can be so sad at times. Besides, I see enough as a police officer. The media is always quick to show one teenager killing another, a teenager arrested for drugs or gang violence. Wouldn't it be great to see a news story about teens out in the community doing positive acts of kindness? So, I reached out to a couple of news stations to see if they would cover this event in which youth were giving back to those in need through the works of Theragood Deeds.

My mind was reeling with all the holidays that we could go out and do good; Valentine's outreach at a nursing home, playing bingo and eating gumbo with the residents; Beat the Heat for Houston's Homeless in June, passing out cold water to the homeless in the hot summer, Thanksgiving outreach as well as Veterans Day at the shelter; Christmas giving gifts to less fortunate families with kids and an Easter Egg Hunt with the kids at the park in April. Don't forget the "Real Talk with Youth" and Back to School supply giveaway event in August before school starts. Outreach with the youth impacting others throughout the city doesn't get any better than that. Not to mention this was all God's plan and the purpose He had for me.

Together we are so much stronger, and the kids did a wonderful job at our first event. ABC13 News was there to catch it all and interview some of the kids. I couldn't ask for anything else that would bring me this much joy but to do it every year. What a blessing to show the city of Houston how Theragood Deeds and youth impacted the homeless community! What a fantastic way to demonstrate how our teens can be and are more than what they have been labeled or what we typically see in the news, violence, drugs, disrespect, death. It was so awesome seeing one

of our young 10-year-olds on television telling everyone
her reason for giving, how happy it makes her feel, and
how it shows that someone cares for them. Think of how
many youths have been inspired to want to do the same.

I was so inspired to keep going and never stop. The
many calls and text messages blasting through my phone
about the amazing job the youth did in giving back to the
homeless meant a lot to them. No violence, no arrests,
no bad vibes coming from the local news stations at that
moment, nothing but youth doing important things in the
community, as I prayed for. Like when you are playing
your favorite sport and looking forward to practicing, I
wanted youth to become motivated and look forward to
serving communities.

December was right around the corner and it was
already time to put together an outreach for Christmas.
As a youth organization, I was looking forward to this time
of giving back to less fortunate kids. But now, here comes
the hard part, where do I get the gifts from? It was time to
put all the not-asking-for-help concepts behind and start
asking folks to contribute. I was able to get donations from
the public and friends. Now, all we needed was a location
for the kids to wrap the gifts and for folks to drop off the
toy donations. But God already had this planned out too!
The city approved us using the park and we had plenty of
volunteers to help. I wanted this Christmas to be so special
for the families that I decided to dress up as Santa Claus
and the kids were going to dress up as elves and deliver
them to each family's home. Thanks to people out in the

community, we were able to deliver wrapped toys to 20 families! We were so happy to put smiles on everyone's faces and warming their hearts.

Keys to Success:

Don't get discouraged if your vision doesn't come true when you want it to but be patient and it will come when you least expect it.

Know that nothing is impossible, but everything is possible when you do what you love and appreciate the life you've been given.

Always be thankful for what you have and never take life for granted.

HOMELESS OUTREACH TEAM

> *"Whoever is generous to the poor lends to the lord, and he will repay him for his good deed." ~ Proverbs 19:17 (ESV)*

When I joined the police department, my goal was to make sure I could make a difference in someone's life, even if they were getting arrested for a crime. I wanted them to learn from it. But of course, I didn't like arresting people. I'd rather another officer makes the arrest while calling me to de-escalate the situation and calm the chaos down. I want to help folks. When I heard that the Houston Police Department was hiring for an officer in the Homeless Outreach Team Unit, I knew that this was definitely for me. I quickly applied to join the team. People told me the best way to show them that you're interested is to do a 30-day rotation with the team. I reached out to a friend and before I knew it, I was doing a 30-day rotation with them. This was a unique group of officers who rarely use their handcuffs but used their hearts to help a homeless person get off the streets. Instead of people running from us, they were running toward us. I was so shocked and never thought I'd ever see this coming. This was amazing and a huge change from what I was used to. I was able to be me and do what I do best when I'm not in uniform and that's smile at everyone and make sure everyone is ok. I now help people get off the streets and sometimes into their own homes. After doing this 30-day rotation, I waited and waited for the position to post.

Serving in my city in this capacity was a new reality for me. The outpouring of love we received from the neighborhood residents was shocking and a big switch from the usual reaction. When we pulled up in the giant "Shamu" Sprinter Van, people waved and smiled at us, reaffirming that it was possible to develop a relationship of trust and respect with the police. I knew that this was the right place for me, and I prayed and prayed that my plan was in-line with God's. Before you know it, they accepted my transfer, and I was officially part of the team.

Keys to Success:

Find what you have a passion for and use it to serve others.

Building relationships is a great way of making an impact in someone's life.

A smile can brighten someone's day. So, smile because it might just brighten your own day.

HUMBLED

> *"Humility is not thinking less of yourself; it's thinking of yourself less." ~ C. S. Lewis – British author and theologian*

It felt like a dream. In 2018, I received an email from the Houston Texans Football Team stating that I was being honored with the "Star of Courage Award." Is this for real? This was an award reserved for first responders, peace officers, firefighters, and emergency medical personnel who show excellence in leadership, bravery, and commitment to Houston. I was struck by all the people in the city who could have been honored for their unbelievable efforts risking their lives every day and putting people first, and word on the street was that I was chosen unanimously. The Texans staff stated that it made that year's selection easy due to all the votes I had, something they had never seen before. They offered to give me tickets to the game and to allow me to hang out during the pregame on the field. I was so excited, but the only thing I could say was this was all God's plan. They also wanted to host an exclusive luncheon for me at the police station, and I was able to invite whomever I chose to come out and join the fun. And that still wasn't it! Since the Texans were playing the Giants, they also brought out NFL retired stars from both teams to pass out signature footballs to everyone; and they gave me a football helmet signed by New York Giants Quarterback Eli Manning. I gave his helmet to my dad, who loved football, and deserved it more than me. I was able to bring my whole organization and youth to the game, where they all had their own section to sit in. Finally, they showed a big picture of our whole team on their mega screen and things we've done in the community in front of the 80,000 plus people at the opening home game. They also honored me with the "Star of Courage Award." I was given a standing ovation, and I happily waved my thanks to everyone. This was truly a blessing from God. This was as small as a mustard seed for Him, but to me, this was huge. I couldn't imagine what it would look like if He were to bless me with something more than that.

I received numerous awards for my work with the youth and in serving the homeless community. Funny, though, that it seems to me that the more I did for the youth and for the city, the more the community awarded me for it. But the whole time, I was thinking I'm only doing what I told God that I wanted to do, and I guess this is how He wants me to be recognized. With every award I've received, I make sure He is recognized for making me who I am and giving me the strength to follow the path that He has laid out for me. When I walk inside my home, I'm amazed to see all those awards and pictures on my wall, reminding me of playing sports as a kid. I finally realized that sports for me were temporary but saving someone's life was meant for me forever.

I don't do what I do for the recognition, but it is amazing to be recognized for following what God has asked me to do. Although my dreams and aspirations included playing on the big court, wowing the crowds with my incredible ball-handling skills, God had other plans for me. I also know that God used sports such as basketball as an analogy for my life. Playing the point guard position my whole life, I was the leader of every team I ever played on, and now I realize that this was all God's plan, preparing me to be a leader for the youth and people in the community. Your life may not be what you want it to be, and you may have made some poor decisions in your life. I want you to know that it is not too late to turn your life around, to follow the path that has been laid out for you, and to reap the many blessings that await. If I learned anything from my years playing sports, nothing comes easy. However, I will do #watevaittakes to reach my goals, find my purpose, and be everything God has planned for me to be. And you can too!!

When I leave this earth, I want to be remembered for being a great police officer who found his purpose by

becoming an advocate for the youth and making a difference in the community. Think about how you want to be
remembered. What do you want people to say about you
when you leave this earth? You do not have to be satisfied
or accepting of the mistakes that you made in the past.
You can choose to look at the world through a different
lens, use the "what if" tool to make better decisions, and
set goals for yourself to follow the path that God has laid
for you. I am here to tell you that just because you have
a history or a past riddled with mistakes, does not mean
that you must resign yourself to one lifestyle or to continue
down that path. You have an option to do #watevaittakes
to take control of your destiny.

Keys to Success:

If you never set any goals nor make any
attempts to achieve them, you will never know
your potential to exceed them.

Never stop dreaming BIG, believing, or pushing
toward what you believe is God's plan for your
life.

Think about how you want to be remembered.

As the saying goes, "It's better to have tried and failed than failing to try!" I want to encourage you to keep pushing forward, work hard, and build on the lessons you have learned along the way. Everyone has a dream, a desire to be more. You must follow that dream, although the path may not be easy or may not lead where you thought it would. But you must dream nonetheless and keep trying. Nothing happens if you sit back and do nothing!

THERAGOOD DEEDS

TheraGood Deeds is a 501(c)3 non-profit organization whose primary focus revolves around assisting inner-city youth, also known as Our Future Achievers, to become positive and affluential members of our society. The organization's name stems from my last name, Theragood. The addition of Deeds was necessary as it reflects the positive standard that I base my life on every day. The dream of Theragood Deeds, Inc was born during my tenure as a Harris County Juvenile Detention Officer. While working at the detention center, I often encountered troubled youth who, after a little positive reinforcement, began to confide in me about their dreams and aspirations. At that moment, I realized it was the job of adults such as myself to offer hope to adolescents who had somehow lost their way. A good deed is defined as the act of kindness, accommodation, generosity, or charity, performed with the simple intention of being helpful. Every day I challenge myself, as well as others, to perform a Good Deed. I did so by forming a Youth Outreach Team. It can be as simple as giving the elderly a helping hand, encouraging someone to keep pushing forward, providing meals to the homeless, or participating in charitable marathons. I also wanted to do more by being engaged one-on-one with the youth. I knew that starting a mentorship program would give them another outlet to go to if there is anything the Mentee needs guidance for and any resources to help them for their future. I believe there are plenty of positive attributes in one's life or community that can be used to maintain a positive outlook. With the assistance of our volunteers, we challenge our future leaders to always think positively and perform Good Deeds not only for themselves but also for society. We also challenge our young leaders to set short-term and long-term goals by identifying and accomplishing their aspirations one good deed at a time.

#WATEVAITTAKES

As part of the outreach program and Theragood Deeds, I am now taking on more risk. My reputation precedes me, and people often call me to talk to their troubled sons and daughters. I get to guide these young people, hold them accountable, and follow up with them as they navigate the hills and valleys of life. I also created a mentor program to help school administrators implement programs in their buildings.

I went through many things in my life and learned so much along the way. I have to say, I went through all of it to ultimately find my purpose. Although my heart was originally guided by the desire to play professional basketball, I know that I have achieved and received so much more by following the purpose God had laid out for me more than anything that I could have defined on my own.

Theragood Deeds, Inc. will be my mark on the world. We serve the communities and the kids, and I am always

willing to do #watevaittakes to make a difference in someone's life. My team and I have even created three short
films to enhance teenagers' lives and provide them with
invaluable information about Choices, Teen Pregnancy,
and Bullying.

Remember the grassroots program I started, "Real
Talk with Youth and Back to School Supply Giveaway?"
Although I only had 18 participants at the very first event,
I am proud to say that we filled 175 seats and standing
room only at our last one. I plan to continue to do #wate-
vaittakes to expand the outreach, promote our events,
and reach kids wherever they are. We even started our
own brand of sweatshirts, hats, and similar wear, which
represents the organization's motto and more importantly,
the philosophy that I have lived by and will continue to do
so #watevaittakes. The goal is to encourage kids to keep
on grinding, continue pushing forward, and never give
up on reaching their goals.

I never had a backup plan as I dreamed big and only
set my sights on playing professional basketball. It wasn't
until life threw a curveball at me and I didn't make the
team that I realized the importance of having a backup
plan. Having just one goal in life is not going to get you
where you need to be since life is all about dreams, challenges, and of course, changing direction. I realized that
just like in basketball, the game of life could suddenly
change unexpectedly. Although the coach may have had a
defensive strategy to prevent the other team from scoring,
he always has a backup plan available if needed.

As I now travel to many schools and speak to young people throughout Texas, I always encourage them to dream big and have a backup plan. I expanded my view of the world, and I understood that there was more to life than basketball and that God had His own plan for my life. I learned from my mistakes and made it my goal to share this information and help others. I want to encourage you to be prepared for whatever life has in store for you, but more importantly, to do #watevaittakes, even if that means stepping outside of your comfort zone to reach your goals and take hold of the life that God has planned for you.

I live by this and hope that through my story, my life's journey, and insight that I have inspired you to do #watevaittakes to find your purpose.